Bridge To Change

Bridge To Change

A Transformation Process For Sustainable Life Fulfillment

Tom Marino

All Rights Reserved. No portion of this book may be reproduced, stored in a retrieval system, or transmitted in any form or by any means-electronic, mechanical, photocopy, recording, scanning, or other-except for brief quotation in critical reviews or articles, without the prior permission of the publisher.

Published by Game Changer Press, LLC DBA Game Changer Publishing

ISBN 9798639037337

www.GameChangerPublishingUSA.com

Dedication

To Kristen, Andrew and Madelyn for all of your love,

support and encouragement

DOWNLOAD YOUR FREE GIFTS

Read This First

Just to say thanks for buying and reading my book, I would like to give you a free bonus gift that will add value and that you will appreciate, 100% FREE, no strings attached!

To Download Now, Visit:

http://www.bridgetochangebook.com/TM/freegift

Bridge To Change

A Transformation Process For Sustainable Life Fulfillment

Tom Marino

www.GameChangerPublishingUSA.com

Table of Contents

Foreword 1

Introduction 7

CHAPTER 1- Surveying the Landscape: The Discovery 17

CHAPTER 2- Beginning the Excavation: Self-Exploration 33

CHAPTER 3- Examining the Blueprints: Values, Beliefs and Fears 47

CHAPTER 4- Building the Foundation: Creating Your Desire Driven Goals 63

CHAPTER 5- Building the Bridge: Preparing for the Change Work 75

CHAPTER 6- Different Vehicles that Cross the Bridge: Change as a Spectrum 85

CHAPTER 7- There's Roadwork on the Bridge: Blocks and Obstacles 91

CHAPTER 8- Crossing the Bridge: Incremental Action Steps 101

CHAPTER 9- Paying the toll: The Value of Your Work 109

CHAPTER 10- Continuing the Journey: Sustaining the Change 119

BONUS CHAPTER- The SMARTER Method for Setting Priorities and Resolving Issues 125

FREE BONUS GIFT 130

Foreword

Change.

/CHanj/ is the act or instance of making or becoming different.

We all know the meaning of the word change. We all know that we want change whether it be our weight, our health, a better job or to improve our relationships. What we often lack is the knowledge of how we enact change. We have to be open and willing to change and must acknowledge that everything happens in our lives for a reason and that all people we meet and situations we encounter are all building blocks to change.

Nevertheless, one thing is for sure. We cannot make these changes on our own. Yes, we are the ones going through the change but we often need guidance on how to get there. We need to learn that the path to change is in all of us, we just need help to unlock the answers. We need guidance! I like to think of change as being made up of a pilot and a navigator, much like in an airplane. The pilot knows how to fly the plane but without proper navigation (or guidance), the plane will fly aimlessly through the skies. The same is true for me when it came to change. I knew I wanted to be on a different path, emotionally, spiritually and even physically. I knew what I wanted but I had absolutely no path or guidance on how to make that change a reality. This is where the intersection of Tom entering into my life took hold.

I met Tom in 2015 at a friend's house during Halloween. The kids were all running around and the parents congregated in the kitchen. Tom and I had an instant connection (albeit through our beloved NY Mets) as we were watching them in the Playoffs. I knew from that night that Tom would be a good friend, someone to hang out with and to go catch a Mets game. What I didn't know was that Tom would change my life forever. I don't make that statement lightly.

Through our many conversations about life, work and family, I opened up about needing change in my life. My perspective in life was off, my work and life balance were tilted too far on the work side and I lacked fulfillment in my day to day routine. I was looking for more. I was looking for a connection.

One where I was unlocking all of the things that I needed to feel fulfilled and improve the areas in my life that I felt needed improvement. One of the main things that I have learned from Tom is that change is subtle. Change takes commitment. Change takes perseverance. And most of all, the change was in me! To know that I was the change was really impactful learning for me. Tom's method unlocked the answers in me I didn't know I had. He taught me to define my goals. Big or small they may be, it doesn't matter. Identifying them was the key.

The first step that Tom (my navigator of change) taught me was to identify the steps I thought it would take to achieve those goals. Next, he taught me to define the actions to take those steps and to hold myself accountable in following through with those steps. Change was at the other end of each of those steps for me. We all want change to be quick and painless. It is not like that, though. Change itself is transformative. It is uncomfortable and inevitable. When opening yourself up to change, everything about you will change along with it. Tom helped me change my outlook on things towards the brighter side. I began posting positive messages on social media. It really helped me to put into the universe all of the positive things I wanted in return. And man did it ever work! People started coming up to me to let me know that not only have they seen the change in me, but my positive posts have had a profound impact on them as well. My goal was not to improve others in this instance (remember, I'm the pilot here). What I didn't realize is that I was becoming the navigator to others in my life! Remember, change is subtle. One goal I had was to improve my health. I made the same excuses we all make - "I'm tired", "I have to work too late", "I'm never going to get back in shape". Tom asked me what I must do to fit my time in for working out. We agreed that I should leave work at 5:00 pm (having already worked nine hours) so that I could get home in time to eat dinner with my family (improving my family connection) and would then have time for my exercise bike (improving my physical and mental health). It was amazing to me that Tom unlocked two very important changes within me that I so desperately wanted and needed only by making me ask myself some key questions and helping me put an attainable plan into place to make it happen. This small change seemed impossible to me before Tom helped me unlock that change.

What Tom made me most aware of is that the universe is telling us what to do. It is putting people in our lives for a reason and it is putting us in situations for a reason. A heightened awareness will absolutely happen during your transformation.

We have to be aware of these things so that we can respond to the signs. We also have to look for the lesson in each situation. The lesson teaches us how to handle things in the future in the best way possible and what we can change about how we use the lesson in our journey. Inside this book are these core principles and more that will lead you to your growth, your success and your own bridge to change. I am so excited for you to learn everything Tom has to offer. If you get to experience what I have with the teachings from Tom, you are in for an amazing, life-changing journey!

Michael Smith

Introduction

In high school, I was told that my dreams were "unrealistic, intangible, and impossible to accomplish. They lacked security and stability. They were not achievable."

If I believed what I was told, I would not be here writing the introduction to this book to assist you across your bridge to change. I have walked across that bridge and if I hadn't, I would not believe that everybody has the ability to create his or her own reality and the life they want for themselves. I would not think it was possible to have a job that I don't see as work. Because I love what I do as a coach. I love the people I get to meet along the way as I assist them through their transformation. My hope for you is that after you read this, you will begin your own journey towards changing your life to a better way of living and loving your life, work and relationships.

First, thank you for allowing me to be a part of your journey. I am Tom Marino and I am your life coach across the bridge to change. As a kid, I was always interested in helping others. I thought I would become a psychologist because of my love for human behavior. I think my desire to help others originated from being raised by a family with traditional values of being there for your family whenever they needed you. The door was always open at my house.

To give yourself in service to others was something to strive towards. I was raised with deep roots in the Church and therefore, I was always involved with something in the Church. Whether as an altar server, a singer in the youth choir or attending youth group, my life revolved around the church and the ideals of service to others. It was important to have something to believe in, that was my faith. I didn't always understand what that meant but I figured it out along my journey.

When I was a teenager, I can remember being the person that people came to for advice. For some reason, people sought me out when they were stuck, when they were struggling and when they were having a difficult time. I always felt the most fulfilled when I gave somebody advice and they benefited from my assistance. That's where my journey really started.

Like many, I was raised to go to school, get good grades, go to a good college and graduate with a degree. Then get a good-paying job, get married, buy a house, raise a family and provide for them. Now, these are not necessarily bad beliefs or ideas, however, there is a key idea missing from this ideology. Life is not a process to follow. It is a series of experiences and choices we make that determine our next steps. No two people have the same life. Sometimes we need a little help in figuring that out. I tried to follow the process but struggled at several points. I was an excellent student throughout the majority of my academic career, but that success did not always lead to happiness or fulfillment. I had been so diligent on the process throughout high school; however, my college days would be the time when I started to determine "my" path.

I entered college bright-eyed thinking that I would become a psychologist because I wanted to help people. I had a passion for understanding how the brain works. I wanted to help other people who were experiencing depression and those who were dealing with anxiety because I had my own anxieties in life. I lived with it – a lot. What I learned later on in life is that anxiety is just misdirected energy and when we don't use it the way it's meant to be used, it takes over and makes us more overwhelmed. I wanted to help people with anxiety to redirect that energy and guide them in a better direction. I double-majored in Psychology and Biology but I did not become a psychologist.

Instead, I decided to pursue medicine. However, it was in this pursuit of going to medical school that I was told for the second time that I was being unrealistic. I was told I didn't have what it took to be a physician. I doubted my abilities. At that time, I also learned about an up and coming profession in medicine that I decided to pursue. That was to become a Physician Assistant. Now, some may say I played it safe, or that I was not good enough for medical school, but I say becoming a PA was the best thing that could have happened to my journey.

What I learned was that I needed to pave my own way. I committed to following a path to medicine because I wanted to understand how we are built. I was intrigued by illness and disease, why it happens and how to fix it. I could help people improve their health and their minds. I wanted to bring hope and healing to others.

I find how hope is sometimes missing when I work with my clients. There is something happening, whether a loss of a job, a loved one, a relationship or loss of direction, hope is missing. I like to restore hope.

I will never forget a patient of mine, we will call him Paul, who was 42 years old, and he had come in for an annual exam. I reviewed his lab results and saw that his prostate levels went from 0.5 to 1.2 in a matter of a year. As a reference in both situations, you wouldn't be too suspicious of anything; however, my gut told me something didn't make sense. I sent him for a sonogram and it was discovered that he had prostate cancer. I will never forget that expression on his face when he said to me, "You saved my life" and that I had given him hope for the future. All I did was follow my instincts and that has always served me well.

Yet part of me was not fulfilled in that practice of medicine. I think it had to do with the culture where I was working. Health care, as you may know, or have heard, is a very difficult profession to work in. It had gotten even more difficult over the last 20 years since I graduated. When I was struggling in my role, I heard the voice of the people who said my goals were unrealistic and unachievable. It created self-doubt.

Fast forward to 2007, I took a leap of faith to change my career track. I answered an ad in the NY Times and I got my first job in administration working for a federally qualified health center in Manhattan, working with people who are underserved, who are mission-driven, people who really believe that healthcare is a right and not a privilege and helping everyone who is in need.

Over the course of my career, I have learned that one of the most important things is to meet people where they are and to help them through their process. I remember overhearing a conversation between a homeless patient and a physician. She was trying to convince him to take his medications for HIV and he said, "I understand that this is important, but my priority is figuring out where I am sleeping tonight and how to get my next meal." That conversation stayed with me for a long time. Our perspective is often different from those who we are trying to help. This reinforced in me the importance of meeting people where they are on their journey.

Over the course of 10 years in healthcare administration, I have had many great experiences that shaped who I am today. However, a few years ago, one of those experiences reshaped my entire life. I was looking for a different work opportunity outside of nonprofits and had accepted a job, but within 60 days, I left it.

It wasn't the right job for me, but the experience happened to push me out of my comfort zone. For the first time in my life, I left something without having anywhere to go to and not being able to work in a place that was going to bring me the fulfillment that I had hoped for was very scary. I said to myself "I have a wife; I have two children, a home, a mortgage and bills." I was faced with unemployment for the first time in my life.

This was probably the most critical moment in my life and it transformed me forever. I left a job and was about to celebrate my 40th birthday. The events that transpired after changed me and brought me from who I was to who I am today. Six months prior to my birthday, I began experiencing a spiritual awakening. I was more aware of things happening around me and my intuition kicked in very strongly. I started trusting my gut more than ever. I began meditating and grounding myself to be more open to the things happening to me. I kept seeing messages on social media about serving your purpose, shining your light and living your true self. It was about having faith and trusting in the universe. It was guidance that I felt I was receiving to move forward.

This is what motivated me to move forward to change and create my reality. It was time to take back control and create my destiny. I told myself, "You are going to do something powerful. You are going to do something where you will take control of the situation." That's what I did. I started my own consulting business. I reached out to a former boss of mine who was looking for someone to do some consulting work. She hired me. During that time, I also made changes to my health and diet. I lost the stress weight and lost almost 30 pounds in 4 months. I was happy, it felt great.

A few months later, I received a notification on LinkedIn that a former colleague, now CEO, was celebrating a work anniversary. We had not connected in a while, but trusting my gut, I reached out, offered congratulations for the anniversary and told her that I was doing some healthcare consulting work. She wrote back and she said, "We actually are looking for a healthcare ops consultant right now - would love to talk to you about it more!" We began working together again.

This experience taught me to put myself out there, to trust in the universe and understand that all will be taken care of as long as you put the effort forward and listen to your gut. This is the place where the universe speaks to you. The thing that keeps you out of danger. The thing that protects you. All you have to do is listen and have a little trust and faith.

When you turn the dial of your mind to "Positivity", you take control of your reality and construct the reality that exists. That is one of the reasons why I became a life coach-to empower people to change their reality and to understand that you have control over your destiny. Things happen to us. We don't always understand why, but we are being prepared for something down the road. It is important to trust your gut and how you choose to respond when things happen. It's our response to them that gives us the control or takes that control away.

So when did I decide to become a coach? I was meditating one day and I asked a question of what I should do next, and I heard "Life Coach". My natural abilities to listen, offering good advice, love for process and desire to serve others were things that shaped my decision to be a Life Coach. Through researching, I realized that it was the next step for me. It was in line with my values. That is why I am here. It is my purpose to serve as a Life Coach to assist people in navigating their lives.

The universe kept finding ways to push me out of my comfort zone. Each of these experiences kept pushing me to grow which I needed to discover my true purpose. The best things have happened to me since then. I have been blessed to meet the most amazing people in my clients. I have watched them transform, take control of their realities, create their realities and be successful.

I coach because I want to empower people to transform their lives and take over their realities and create the reality that they want. This is a journey. It's a process. It's a process of moving out of your comfort zone, about evaluating beliefs and values. In the process, there is healing. Healing is probably the most important thing that comes out of life coaching. It's about taking the things that hold you back, that don't allow you to take the leap. It's a stripping away of old beliefs. It allows you to get rid of those obstacles and face your fears head-on so that you can move forward. My mission is to help you become empowered to transform your reality, to live your truth and find a more fulfilling and happier life. My guarantee is when you put the work in; you will raise your level of self-awareness and gain many new perspectives.

Let's get you moving to living the life that you want to live!

CHAPTER 1

Surveying the Landscape: The Discovery

Before we proceed to your first session, the first chapter of this book, let us set some expectations:

1. Coaching requires that you have a desire to make a change or changes in your life.
2. You must be motivated to start making those changes now.
3. Change takes time and is a process.
4. You must do the work and put the time in.
5. You must answer questions truthfully and honestly. You must answer each question. Not answering them is avoiding something that you don't know is holding you back.
6. When you are stuck, don't give up. Start again.

7. I am cheering you on to make the changes that you want to make.
8. Lastly, hold yourself accountable and if you struggle with that, then reach out to me, that's my job as your coach...to hold you accountable.

Let's begin...

The first session in your coaching experience is an opportunity to survey your landscape, more formally known as the discovery. The goal of this discovery is to identify the issues that you want to work on. That you want to change. Sometimes, clients seek me out to help them for one reason like a career change and before we know it, the real issue is their relationship with their significant other. But that's the purpose of the discovery.

It is an opportunity for me to really get to know my clients. For my clients, it is an opportunity to peel away the things that are holding them back, leave them stuck, and identify what they really want to change.

By the end of most sessions, we have about 15 issues or topics that may need to be worked on. But it's up to you as the client to determine which ones you want to start with.

I love getting to know my clients in this session because it really makes the work that we do together more meaningful. I come to understand your perspectives, your values, and what you need in order to move forward and be successful.

So how do I help you get started? It's simple, I'll ask you to rate the following areas of your life on a scale of 1 to 10, one being that you are not happy with the way things are and 10 being that you love how things are in that area of your life. The survey includes the following areas in your life:

- Friendships
- Family
- Significant other
- Career
- Physical Environment
- Physical Health
- Emotional Health
- Balance in Life
- Finances

- Spirituality/Religion
- Education
- Personal Growth
- Personal Time

Once you have rated these areas in your life, I'll ask you to discuss the areas where you rated an 8, 9, or 10 first. Then we move down to the lower ratings. The reason I want to start with the more positive areas of your life is to determine and understand what attributes are present that make them so successful for you. It's these attributes that become the foundation to build upon in the areas that you want to make the changes.

For example, I was working with a client and we were talking about her friendships and family. She had rated them an 8 and 9, respectively. I asked her to provide three adjectives to describe what made her rate this high. Her three words were honesty, respect, and love.

It was therefore very predictable that when we finally discussed her relationship with her spouse, which she rated a 3, that the opposites of these words were the ones she used to describe her significant other. She felt disrespected, unloved, and that her husband was dishonest with her. During our work together, she had chosen to work on her relationship. So I asked her, "What do you need to move your rating from a 3 to 5 and then a 7?" And her answer was, "honesty, respect, and love."

That's what gives us the core of what we are going to work on in our coaching relationship. In our sessions, we will work on moving that rating up - discovering ways for her to find what she is looking for in her relationship.

This is what the discovery is all about.

In the process of surveying the landscape, I often learn many things about my clients. The first thing I like to understand is where their level of consciousness resides. I studied Neuro Linguistic Programming (NLP) and have my certification. In NLP, it is important to understand the 4 levels of consciousness, also thought of as our levels of responsibility. They are:

- Level 1 = life happens to me
- Level 2 = life happens for me
- Level 3 = life happens through us
- Level 4 = life happens as us

So if you live in level 1, you take no responsibility for your life and you blame everything on someone or something other than you. In level 2, we take responsibility, we give up blame and we empower ourselves. If you live in level 3, you have found purpose and allow yourself to be guided by your purpose. Level 4 means that we have given our soul over to a higher power and that we will be guided to serve the greater good.

So where do you live? Level 1, 2, 3 or 4?

Well, if you have picked up this book, you are living right now in level 2. You are taking responsibility for your life and empowering yourself.

It is easier for all of us to point a finger at someone or something else than it is to point it at ourselves. Part of freeing yourself to change is to be able to take accountability for your actions and empower yourself to make that change. When we take the perspective of "life happens to me" (I like to call it 'the woe is me'), we don't grow and move beyond our comfort zone. Being in the negative is where many people like to live because it's easier than dealing with having to do something about it to make it better.

I like to refer to level 2 as the *"FOR YOU* MOVEMENT" because when we look at it, you have already identified that what is happening *FOR YOU* is an opportunity to grow and move out of your comfort zone. This is how you empower yourself. This is what you need to move forward in coaching to make the changes you desire to make. If you believe life happens to you, you remain stuck and your comfort zone doesn't expand.

I was working with a client and she told me a story about an elderly woman that she knows. The lady is in her 80's and was at her cabana at the beach. My client rents the cabana immediately next to hers. One day they were both leaving and the woman fell and really got hurt. My client came to her coaching session very upset saying, "Why does this always happen to me?" Now, she had been a caretaker for her own parents who had experienced their fair share of falls, but she asked me why this happened to her. I said to her "Why wouldn't this happen to you? It happened for you. You were right where you needed to be. You were there for the lady but it also happened for you." In that moment, the light bulb went on. She had just moved from level 1 to level 2.

When you engage in a coaching relationship with me or another life coach, you engage in a process that happens for you.

It pushes your boundaries. It holds you accountable. I said in my introduction, this is about increasing your self-awareness. This is about improving who you are. It's about gaining a new perspective.

Another important thing that comes out of the discovery is the understanding of how people see their locus of control. Understanding your locus of control is extremely important in the change process.

The locus of control is either internal or external. Sometimes it is situationally dependent and therefore can be seen on a spectrum. If you have an internal locus of control, you recognize that you can manage a situation, that you have the ability, the power, and the strength to take on controlling the matter. If you have an external locus of control, you allow external factors to determine your level of control.

When people speak, you can hear in their language their locus of control. There are people who walk around saying "I can do this" when they are faced with a situation, task or problem. These people see their control as internal. On the other side, people who say, "I can't" in response to a situation are externally oriented in regards to control.

When I hear my clients say, "I can't", I ask, "What can you do?" That is part of how we begin to take your control back. It's what allows you to begin seeing a different perspective.

During the discovery, I also gained an understanding of how to work best with my clients. It is important for me to understand introversion and extroversion. It is very important to understand people's motivation and motivators. Introverted individuals get their energy from themselves, so often motivation comes from within.

On the other hand, extroverts are people who get their energy from the outside world and from other people. When you go to a party, you will see the extroverts having conversations with many different people because they are getting that energy and they are feeding off the energy of somebody else.

To embark across the bridge of change, we have to recognize where our control, energy, and motivation are coming from. When I'm working with someone, I know that what works for the extrovert is not going to work for someone who is introverted. That's an important part to understand and realize as a coach.

If you feel as though the external world is controlling things for you, it is going to be very hard to step out of that and move from level 1 to level 2. In order to empower change in yourself, you have to be able to remove the blame and reduce the external factors that contribute to your sense of control.

However, whether introverted or extroverted, both reach out to coaches for assistance. The introverts come because they are struggling to find motivation in themselves. The extroverts come because they have too many things happening for them and they need someone to help them organize their issues.

It is important to acknowledge what is influencing us. Whether we are an introvert or an extrovert, we can be influenced and internalize false realities. Social media is the epitome of false realities. 'Fakebook' forces people to constantly compare themselves to others. It increases the opportunity for scrutiny and judgment. When we take on someone else's life, we start asking ourselves, "Why doesn't that happen for me?" This is where many people become unhappy and lose a sense of control. But we have control...we have to take it back, focus on us, and only worry about ourselves.

So what is going to make you feel more fulfilled? This is the essence of what we are trying to get out of this discovery session. What do you desire to change?

Do you want a new career, a new job? Do you want new friendships? Does your relationship with your family, spouse, partner or child need to change?

People come to coaching and think that they're going to change other people or they're going to change the relationship. Oftentimes, by the time the discovery session ends, clients have realized that the thing they need to change the most is themselves and their perspectives. They have to recognize that the change that needs to take place is in them. That is our motivation if we want to make ourselves better. We have to change how we are.

Another important aspect of the discovery is that sometimes change happens for us, and we are responding to the changes that happen as opposed to having the desire to make the change. For example, we may be thrust into change by losing a job, experiencing a loss, being forced to retire earlier than expected, or your spouse tells you they want a separation or divorce. These are all major life transitions that are happening for you. It is difficult to find the motivation to continue the change once they have started. In chapter 6, we will discuss the change spectrum, but for the purposes of the discovery, it is important to understand the type of change that is happening.

When change happens for us, it can be difficult. However, we need to acknowledge that one of the constant things in the world is change. It is important to have the conversation that when change happens, what determines the outcome is how we approach and respond to that change. Often, when people are thrust into change, they become overwhelmed and often experience loss of control. They slip into the 1st level of consciousness but then realize that they have to act.

I tell my children every time they make a mistake or don't perform well that I am not so concerned about what they did, but more concerned about how they respond to it. I am not focused on the fact that they didn't do well on the test, I ask them to explain what they are going to do in order to do better next time. In holding ourselves accountable, we must decide what our response is and the action we will take to get there.

So what's changing for you? What's changing in your life? Are you going through a divorce or a separation? Are you being forced to make a career change? Are you afraid of what that means? Are you willing to make a change? The opportunity is happening for you to look in on yourself to make the changes you need to make.

In the last part of a discovery session, we will explore some key aspects that allow understanding where you live spiritually. Do you trust in GOD, a great being, energy, the universe or do you trust yourself? Do you believe that everything is happening for you? Do you believe that this change is happening for you? And do you trust that if you make some changes, good things are going to happen for you? When we trust, we can make the changes that we need to make and make them successfully. Because trusting in the universe, trusting in the power of this is happening for you allows us to move forward and make the change that we want to make. It is important to trust the process.

What are you grateful for? What experiences are you thankful for? Who are the people you are thankful for?

Then I ask when this is all done in 90 days, 180 days and a year from now when you've put in the work and you've made the changes, "Are you grateful for those things that are going to happen?" Because when we put out gratitude and we express gratitude, good things happen. We have to be grateful for the things we have been given and the things that we have yet to be given as if they exist already.

I remember listening to something about Tyler Perry and the person he was before his success. He would tour open houses at mansions and go to dealerships to test drive Maserati's and Porsches. When he would walk into the mansions for an open house, he would look up and say, "I live here". And when he was driving those cars, he would say, "I drive this car".

He put out into the universe and expressed gratitude for those things that would happen before they even happened. He manifested the change.

Are you putting out things that are going to bring you good fortune and abundance later on? Are you grateful for them today, even though you haven't secured them?

Do you believe that people serve a purpose, that everyone serves a purpose for you? Everyone comes into your life for a reason. A friend, a family member, a coach, a teacher and anyone that you meet randomly on the street, they serve some purpose. Do you believe that?

Because in understanding your landscape and discovering more about you, it is about evaluating what you believe and what you find as important. When you understand these things, we start to understand the issues that we need to work on.

As we wrap up the discovery session, we review the issues and life areas that you want to work on. Whether it be your job, finances, relationship with your significant other or something else. You want to work on your physical health and well-being. You want to make changes. Are you motivated? What is your motivation on a scale of 1 to10?

Well, let us be grateful for all the things that you have been given to work on. Let us express gratitude. Let us put it out there and then let us move forward to figuring out how and what you need to do to give you the fulfillment that you want to achieve.

The discovery allows us to set the stage for the work that we are going to do together. One of the things I love about a discovery session is when people come out of that session, whether it's an hour, hour and a half, they have already gained a new perspective about themselves. They have already heightened their awareness of themselves. It is my hope that by this point you have gained some fresh perspective.

> Questions to Consider:
>
> 1. What areas of your life would you rate an 8, 9, or 10?
> 2. What 3 adjectives would you use to describe those areas?
> 3. What areas of your life do you want to see change?
> 4. In the areas of your life that you want to change, what adjectives are missing that exist where things are good?
> 5. What do you need to happen to make the changes you desire to make?

CHAPTER 2

Beginning the Excavation: Self-Exploration

On Friday evenings, I take my son to baseball lessons at a facility run by two former professional baseball players. Every week their dad Ron is there putting his heart and soul into his sons' business. We had a conversation recently where he asked me what I do for a living. I told him I was a life coach.

He proceeded to tell me, "You know, I have never worked a day in my life". I found that statement so powerful. I thought, "He never worked a day in his life, what did he do?"

He said, "I love playing baseball. I always loved being athletic so I became a gym teacher, a baseball coach. Even to this day, I still coach baseball, but I've never worked a day in my life. "This is a man who truly loves what he does. It was a bit surprising that a man who was born in the late '40s, raised with probably very different values, somehow, someway, always found how to be true to himself and to do what he loves. Then he said, "That's how I raised my boys to do what they love. They wanted to play baseball. They played baseball. They did what they love. And they still do what they love every day. Now that they've retired from baseball, they work to develop kids to play the game that they love so much. They help other kids find their love."

That is what the self-exploration process is all about. It is about finding what you love. What is your truth? What are the things that you know about yourself to be so true? What is the thing that you love most?

My son Andrew shared a quote with me by Mark Twain, "The two most important days in your life are the day you were born and the day you find out why." I was struck by this quote, not only because it came from my eleven-year-old son, but also because it is the essence of what your deep dive into yourself is all about.

Do you recognize that the two greatest days in your life are the day you were born and the day you figure out why? That is what most people are looking for. They are trying to find out why they were born. What are they put on the earth to do? What is that something? That something is your truth.

It took me a while to figure that out. Our life purpose is to bring us fulfillment. It is the essence of our soul's truth. Up until my 40th birthday, my purpose was being a husband, a father, a loving and caring person, and someone to serve others. However, I was not fulfilled in my service to others. My purpose was further defined at that time. I realized that I needed to do more and that I WAS here to continue to serve. And even though I struggled to figure out what it was, one of the greatest days of my life was when I made the commitment to become a life coach.

Every day that I coach, I don't work. My coaching is the thing that I love doing the most of any of the roles I have filled, other than being a husband and a parent. It is the reason why I was born. Which is why I want you to figure out why you were born as well.

Let us start by exploring what happens naturally for you.

Everyone has natural abilities and natural gifts. Some people have the natural ability to listen, write or speak. Some people have the natural ability to advise. Others are athletic, musically inclined, creative or artistic. How about you, what comes easily to you?

Are you a good listener? Are you good at giving advice? Do you like organizing things? Do you like listening to people's problems and helping them find a solution?

Are you athletic? Do you like playing sports? Do you like coaching? Do you like coaching your child's team? Do you like being creative and designing web pages or logos? Do you like creating marketing materials? What are the things that come naturally that you really did not have to learn how to do, but just are part of who you are?

In exploring what is natural, we uncover your truth. Part of my truth is that I am good at getting people to open up to me. What is your truth? Are you passionate, intelligent? What do you love? What do you like and aren't sure why? What works for you when you really don't have to put forward much effort?

For Ron, it was his love of baseball, being athletic and following that passion.

That is why he can say that he never worked a day in his life. That is him using his natural abilities to do something that he loves and that brings him fulfillment. So what occurs naturally for you? Take a minute to ponder that. Think about what are the things that come naturally to me that I didn't really have to learn how to do. What am I naturally good at?

Let us now discuss your dreams.

It is important to know your dreams.

What were your dreams when you were a kid? What did you want to grow up to be? Did you want to be an athlete? Did you want to be a magician? Did you want to play football? Did you want to be a ballerina? Did you want to be the person that you are today?

Our dreams are there for a reason. They are the guide to living your truth. I have always dreamed of writing a book. That dream has come true. What did you dream about as a teenager or young adult? Our dreams are there for us. They are our direction in life that we should follow. People abandon their dreams because of 'reality setting in'. We, therefore, don't live our dreams, we abandon them and we live unfulfilled.

What dreams did you give up on or did you follow them? Were you injured and were not able to play the sport that you always wanted? Did it limit you from doing what it is you love to do? If this happened, then what can you do to still live that dream?

We don't have to necessarily live our dream as a way of earning a living, but we need to incorporate aspects of the dream into our life. We need to adjust. If we totally block it out, we are not being true to ourselves. We can make it a hobby. Utilize our dream in being creative or volunteering, - putting it to use.

I often talk about my son and his dream of playing professional baseball. He is a very talented kid. He has an athletic talent that I never had. My wife and I are fostering in him to develop that talent. Not for me, but for him. That's what he wants. He wants to play baseball. He wants to be a major league baseball player. But sometimes when I say to people that my son wants to do that, people think I'm crazy and say, "That's a nice dream. Keep dreaming, that'll never happen."

How do you know that it's never going to happen? Is it because the naysayers say it won't happen? When I let the doubters fill my head, I say to my son, "What happens if you don't make it to the major leagues?" His response is "I'll find something else to do in baseball. But I love that game and I love what I do. I love playing this sport. I love being a baseball player." That's his dream. Who am I to say, "No, that's not a realistic dream for you?"

He realizes that it's going to take work to get to where he wants to go. But that's work he's willing to do. When you love something that you do, you are willing to work for it. That's what I find a lot when people are struggling in their careers. So in the self-exploration process, we talk about the things that you do every day. And I ask, are they things that come naturally to you or are they things you really have to work hard and learn how to do?

Most times, it's something that was hard for them to do. Most times, it was something that didn't come easy. There are unnatural things in people's careers that cause them to become discouraged. It's having work within the politics. It's having to learn how to navigate the corporate culture. It's trying to figure out how to be better than everybody else, how to stand out from everybody else. We live in a world that is very competitive. But if you're not someone who is competitive, it makes it that much harder. So when you think of your life, is it the thing that you dreamt about?

Our goal is to get to living your truth, it is then when you become free. If you're not living your truth, you cannot be free. Being free is being Ron or my son. It's looking at the experiences as never working a day in your life. It's living your dream.

As we explore, we pull out the components and possibilities that exist for you. The purpose is to determine the possibilities for you to research and test out as you move through your transformation to fulfillment.

The next question to ask is: Who do you admire most?

Living or dead, family members, friends, neighbors, colleagues, who do you admire? What are the things that you admire about them? Think about it for a moment. Think about who you admire. Is it your dad? Is it your mom? A movie star or a celebrity? A speaker, a coach, a successful businessperson? What do you admire about them?

Because what you admire about them is the thing that you admire or want for yourself. You often see in them what you see in yourself. They are the reflection in your mirror.

Now complete this sentence, "The me I see in them is _____".

Is it your strength, your confidence, boldness, sense of humor, altruism, caring, loving persona? Is it that they know what they want? Is it the risks they take? For me, the me I see in them is being a risk-taker- I see in them the person who took a leap of faith who had almost nothing left.

Who is the me that you see in them? That's part of exploring who you are.

The next question I would like to ask is:

When was the time in your life that you felt completely satisfied?

Look back at the moments of your when you felt completely satisfied. Most people explain when they're on vacation. I just returned from a trip to Jamaica. On that trip, I was standing on the beach with my feet in the sand as the waves were coming over my feet and immersing me in the oneness of being with the ground. That was extremely satisfying to me. I felt at peace. I felt a sense of oneness with the earth and with nature. Watching the waves brings such peace to me, watching the water come as a wave and then gently caress my feet and bring me deeper into the ground, gives me a sense of oneness. That satisfaction is how I feel being grounded to the world.

What do you do on a daily basis to ground yourself, to make you feel one? It's in that oneness that we feel a sense of inner peace. That inner peace is what we are searching for. Once we find it, that feeling will be present when we are fulfilled. If we have inner peace, we are successful in what we do.

Maintaining inner peace is success. It is very difficult to have peace while living in this chaotic and competitive world full of pushdowns instead of elevating ups. The world may try to squash our possibilities, our hopes, and our dreams, but when we have inner peace, when we feel oneness and satisfaction with the world and we're able to maintain that in the face of being pushed down, then we know we are living our truth and we are free.

So what is it that makes you feel grounded? What is it that makes you feel one with the universe? What is it that makes you maintain your peace?

One of my favorite questions in the process is, what would you do if you had all the time, money, resources and could not fail?

Would you work? Or would you do something else?

The answers to this question always vary. Many people would still work, yet others would do something else. Many clients say that they would travel the world and explore other cultures. They would embark on adventure. So what would you do?

In the second part of the exploration, we acknowledge the things that you've learned over the course of your life: the skills, talents and what you have mastered. What are the things you learned that you are proudest of?

What is your talent or skill?

Everyone has a talent, and if you say, "No, I don't have a talent", of course, you do. It's just not been discovered yet. We put huge expectations on ourselves that you have to play an instrument, be good at sports, or be very good at working with people. We use that as a reason to be talented, but being simply someone who may listen really well or give advice really well, that is your talent.

What do you do really well? What did you learn to do really well? What skill have you developed? Maybe a job you had allowed you to enhance a skill. Maybe you were good at speaking with people but learned customer service skills that enhanced your natural ability. Maybe you are a good organizer. Maybe you are really good at organizing closets and you learned how to better design closets. It's a skill that you now have. It's what makes you unique and different from everyone else. And that is what should make you confident.

So what makes you feel confident? It's often the things that make you feel satisfied, fulfilled, maintained in your inner peace. What have you learned over the course of your life that gives you confidence? Because when you have confidence, you are able to explore more of your possibilities. If you don't have the confidence, you're not going to come out of your comfort zone.

You're not going to take that leap forward. I would have never thought in a million years I'd be sitting here writing this book. I never thought in a million years that I would have the confidence to go out on my own and start my own business. But it is in learning from what I could do that I became more confident in who I am and I want that to happen for you. So what makes you confident? What is your truth? How will you be free?

The goal of this session is to assemble a list of your components and possibilities. Sometimes what comes out of the possibilities is all of the things you can do, be or dream to be. It's often about the lifestyle that you are searching for and the path to it.

Once the list is complete, we set out to test and research the possibilities to become more informed about how they line up for you. We begin to dive into our values, beliefs, and fears that arise in that process. Before we enter into those things, review the key questions from this chapter.

Questions to Consider:

1. What are my natural abilities and skills?
2. What did I dream about becoming as a kid, teenager, young adult or even now?
3. Who do I admire and why?
4. When was a time I was completely satisfied in my life? Describe it. Close your eyes and take yourself there.
5. What would I do if I had time, money, resources and couldn't fail?
6. What skills have I learned over the course of my life? What are my talents?

CHAPTER 3

Examining the Blueprints: Values, Beliefs and Fears

In preparing for the Discovery and Self-Exploration, my clients identify their life values by completing an assessment. In my opinion, the most important thing that we do in life coaching, whatever outcome that we are trying to achieve, whatever the direction we go, we must honor and align the values that you hold as sacred or important for yourself.

People are not always sure of what they value and they know that something is missing. Sometimes they have values that don't align with what they do in their work, their life or in their relationships. Our values also change at different stages. If you don't consider your values and understand what values are important to you, then it's very challenging for us to work together in search of your life fulfillment.

Understanding your values is critical to deciding workplace, living environment and ultimately lifestyle. When you are searching for a new job and you look at a company that you want to become part of, you need to assess the company's values. You need to ensure that the values of that company align with your values. If there is a misalignment, there will be conflict down the road. It's going to make you second guess or think about why you really decided to work for the company.

For example, I have worked for companies that value compassion, being focused on the patient, meeting the patient where they are and working together as a team. If my values did not align with compassion, teamwork and focusing on the patient first, I would be out of alignment and thus may not find fulfillment.

Your values are your recipe for fulfillment. So what do you value the most? What are the five or 10 values that you hold as the most important ingredients to who you are as a person and what you do in your life? For example, your values may be: independence, recognition, acknowledgment, time with family, and a healthy lifestyle. Therefore, it will be important to honor them in your work, your life, and your relationships.

When working with clients that are having challenges in their marriage, they often feel as though they don't know themselves or their spouse. I encourage them to complete a values exercise in an effort to begin understanding each other again.

Karen, a client of mine, is in her early 40's and came to me to help her redefine her career and find what she could do to get back into the workforce. In our discovery, it became apparent that she was really searching for a path to improve her relationship with her husband and discover herself.

Karen is going through a point in her marriage where she's calling into question a lot of her own values and a lot of who she is as a person. One of the things that happened for her is her husband's career success. She is struggling because she feels that she has lost her value in her relationship as an equal partner.

Over the course of their marriage, their "contract"' has changed, but there was no negotiation for that change. When I speak of a contract, it is something that my wife says is part of every marital relationship. For example, the contract is the values and expectations that each of you has for each other. If a couple doesn't re-evaluate that contract from time to time, it evolves without negotiation. The result is conflict in the marriage.

Let us discuss their contract. When they got married, they both had their own careers. They both were successful in their career. They both made about the same amount of money. They were equal contributors to their relationship and to their marriage in the beginning.

Then they had children. When their children came, they suffered from some medical complications. This is where the contract changed. Karen stepped away from her career to become a full-time nurse and mother to their children. Her husband continued to work and provide for them. He continued to excel in his career, being promoted to a senior partner. He works, in her words, "all the time".

She is a mom, a nurse, and a housewife. In discussing this with her, I asked if there was ever a conversation about the expectations for each other. The answer was "no". So fast forward to now, their children are older and thankfully, healthy. However, she is unfilled in her career or lack thereof.

But by being unhappy about her career, she realized she needed to work on herself. She realized the most important things she had to work on were her values. She knows how to succeed, but being out of the workforce for the last 10 years caused her to lose some of her confidence in her own abilities. One of her values is being competent and capable. In fulfilling her roles both at home and at work, she will need to be able to meet these values. Being competent and capable must be present in her relationship with her husband and in their marriage contract.

She comes from a house of traditional Italian values with the ideology of marrying a good man who is a good provider, a husband, and a father. But because her values are not aligned with these beliefs, she is in conflict over what to do.

She is being pushed out of her comfort zone to question her values and beliefs. When we start to question the things that we believe, it is important for us to question the values that we bring to those beliefs.

Beliefs play a very important role for us in order to move forward. It is more important to understand what we believe because oftentimes we just believe something as it is or how it was told to us.

I was working with a client and he is very much stuck in a level one consciousness. In working with him, I asked, "How do you look at success? Because I'm not hearing that you feel as though you're successful." He is in his late 20s, but he was looking at measuring success as "You go to school, you get a good job, you get married, you buy a house, you have a family, you continue to support that family. You do well, you succeed, you retire, and then you die." This was serving as his foundation for success, while repeatedly reinforcing that he was a failure.

I asked him, "Do you believe in this ideology? Is this the only description for success?" He looked at me and he said, "Yeah, that's what I believe." I said, "Is that what you truly believe or what you were told to believe?"

Many are afraid to question their beliefs, to explore outside of their belief system. We have beliefs that are instilled in us and how dare we question those beliefs. But in order for us to move forward and create the changes that we want to create for ourselves, we have to question those beliefs. We have to explore if those things are true and do they match up with the values that we hold now.

Some people will have a set of values that are important to them, like being independent, feeling confident, having a healthy lifestyle. Yet, they may have been raised with a belief that contradicts these.

We have to explore those beliefs and make sure that they are true. When I work with clients, I ask what they believe. When they say they believe something, I ask them what evidence they have to support that belief. So when people are not feeling worthy, loved or respected and they are a 'woe is me' client or they feel as though they have done nothing but fail, I ask them, "Do you believe that you are worthy?" And often in that situation, they will say no. I'll say, "Tell me what evidence you have that says you are not worthy. Every single person in this world is worthy of love, respect, abundance, positive and happy lifestyle."

Everyone is worthy of that. It is in the choices that we make that changes that perspective. But it comes from what our beliefs are. We have to explore what our belief system is. If you don't believe you are worthy, how can you make a change that promotes self-love?

Whenever you look in the mirror and you don't see someone who is amazing, fantastic, or awesome, you have to replace those beliefs. We have to replace the beliefs that are destructive. We have to replace the beliefs that hinder our ability to change. To help replace these beliefs, I encourage my clients to make a list of affirmations.

What are the things that you want to believe about yourself and that you need to affirm daily? It's a little odd in the beginning to say things about yourself that you're striving for, that you hold as sacred for yourself. It's uncomfortable for people who don't do that regularly. But if you don't look in the mirror and say, "I love who I am, I am worthy, I am loved, I am deserving of respect, I am deserving of abundance, I am confident," how can you ever change and move forward in a positive direction?

It starts with you. It starts with your beliefs. It starts with what you value. And the thing that disrupts that is fear.

Fear is the killer of many of these feelings. Fear may validate a belief when you are afraid to challenge that belief. Some of my clients who are single and trying to go back out into the dating scene have a fear of dating because they have a fear of rejection. Well, if you don't feel that you're worthy or deserving of love, how can you accept love? If you have a fear of rejection, you're just validating and providing evidence for the negative, allowing that belief of worthiness to remain.

Is that belief true? It may not be a true belief, but it's the belief that gets validated by the fear. When we validate our beliefs in fear, fear stops us. Fear is what holds us back. My wife often says, "Worry is a bridge that you haven't crossed yet." That's what fear is, a bridge you haven't crossed yet. Crossing the bridge to change will help you to integrate these fears into your life so that you can honor them and acknowledge the role they play in moving forward.

What is fear?

We view fear in making us anxious and worried. It takes away our confidence. We feel as though we're not good enough. Some of us have fears of being alone. Some of us have fears of rejection. People have fears of failure. But what are all of these things? They are all the things that stop us from moving forward and from taking risks.

The perspective that I would encourage you to take is that fear is your friend, not your enemy. Fear gives you information to make decisions cautiously. Fear is the thing that becomes a guiding principle. Fear is the catalyst that pushes you to grow.

I'm working with a gentleman right now; we'll call him Todd. He is struggling with making a career change and leaving his current job in which he's not happy and moving into another job.

But everything he does is rooted in fear. He fears judgment that has made him develop an inability to express himself or to say something that he believes is true. He is worried about what others would say about his opinion. He is afraid of being ostracized, marginalized, disenfranchised because in the past a boss said to him "No, that's not a good idea." I turned to him one day and said, "For every good idea, there are a thousand other ideas that weren't good. We have to try. We can't let fear stop us."

We can integrate fear into what we do. We need to integrate fear into our movement forward. We cannot allow it to hold us back from moving forward. We can use it to be informed. When fear holds us back, change does not happen.

It's a battle of the power of the ego versus the power of the soul. The power of your soul is the thing that gives us intuition. It lives in our gut. To understand your soul you must ask, "What is your gut saying?" Your soul is your compass; it gives you direction and it tells you when something is about to happen, sometimes good, sometimes not. We don't always follow our gut when it comes to making decisions.

We make the decision with our brain, which is the power of the ego. The ego is what gives us the choice. Our soul knows where we need to go, but it's the ego that hijacks our intuition when we decide.

Ego is very important. It is what keeps us grounded in reality. It's what helps us to judge between societal norms and what we're driven to do instinctually, not soul-driven, instinctually driven, biologically driven. The ego fosters fear and anxiety. It takes over the energy of the soul and does not allow the soul to be expressed. The soul represents your truth. Truth is what you feel at your core. If you don't express your soul, you give power to the ego and the choices that you make are going to be most likely based in fear.

Anxiety. I define it as misdirected energy when we are worried about something. It is a bridge we haven't crossed yet. We're looking at something in the future. We're not focused on the here and now. We're letting what we're thinking about in the future disrupt what's happening here in the present.

Take a moment and focus on this moment only. What is happening right now? What are you thinking about at this very moment? Is it the present moment, the past or the future? If you're in the present, you should not have to worry. You should not have fear. You should not have anxiety. If you're thinking about something that's going to happen tomorrow, you're not living in the present. Be here in this moment. Be here right now. That's what the soul is asking you to do. The ego is what's making you see the tunnel between the past and the future. That's where regret, guilt, anxiety, fear, and worry come into play because we're not being present.

When I speak with Todd and I ask him to tell me right now what he is afraid to say at work and he states his opinion about reforming health care, he can do it. He states well. What allows him to do this? The answer is, he's not thinking about tomorrow or what someone else may say. He's thinking about right now; he is being present.

The important thing, when we have struggles between our ego and our soul, is to find a way to keep them balanced. When they are not balanced, it disrupts our ability to move forward. It holds us back; we get stuck.

Another client I've been working with is an executive in the financial world. Steve is struggling in his day job because he feels as though he is in danger of losing his job and that he doesn't have the respect of the people that report to him. Because of a challenging political culture, he doesn't feel comfortable in his environment.

We were having a session where he mentioned that instead of holding a subordinate accountable, he deflected because of the friendship the subordinate has with his boss. I said to him, "What makes you give your subordinates the power? Just because they have a friendship with your boss doesn't mean you have to give them your power. What makes you surrender your power?" It was the fear of repercussions from his boss.

I once heard the comedian, Sarah Silverman say, "'When we are in a survival mode, we don't thrive". She was referring to her grandmother as a struggling immigrant. This was a great statement and so true. If you are living in fear and if your motivation is based in fear, it is not a situation where you're going to thrive. It is not a situation that is going to be productive for you. It is a situation that is only going to continue to be fueled by fear, not progress.

In closing this chapter, it's important that we establish and understand what our values are. Then we should bring those values and question whether our beliefs are in line with our values, and if they are not, we should ask ourselves: What should we do to change our beliefs for them to honor our values? Is it the fear that we have that validates those beliefs and makes those beliefs true? And if we realize that we are responding to our own beliefs out of fear, we are not going to be able to change.

Start evaluating your current beliefs and constructing new beliefs that are true, that are valid for you and honor your values and use the fear as something that informs you but doesn't hold you back. Let it be the thing that you need to integrate into your new beliefs and your values and take that with you to move forward.

So take a moment before moving on to the next chapter and ponder these questions

Questions to Consider:

1. What do you value?
2. What are your beliefs?
3. Do your values honor your beliefs and vice versa?
4. Are your beliefs rooted in fear?
5. Are your beliefs true? If they're not, write some new beliefs.

CHAPTER 4

Building the Foundation: Creating Your Desire Driven Goals

You are now on your 3rd session after completing the Discovery and Self-Exploration sessions. We have cleared the field and dug the hole so we can begin building the foundation for the bridge to change. We take the issues from the discovery and the components and possibilities from your exploration and determine our steps forward.

The goals that you create to begin your transformation must be very clear, well thought out and outcome driven. The goals that we will create in this session will become the foundation for our work together. As we achieve some goals, each new goal we create becomes a piece of the structure for the bridge, whether a support beam, the planks to walk across or a suspension cable.

Sometimes, when people set out to change something, they will set a goal that may be very vague. It may not be sustainable. It could be poorly designed. Then what eventually happens is that we procrastinate on doing the work to achieve the goal or abandon it completely.

For example, think about New Year's resolutions. Everybody makes New Year's resolutions and make goals to change something in their lives. January is the month of optimistic goals that lead to little or no change that is sustainable.

We hear people say that they will lose weight, exercise more, do something better, do something different, do stuff that is going to make them feel better and start the new year on the right foot. Gym memberships often go up in the month of January. I love going to the gym and seeing all the resolutioners- they are always there for the first one, two, almost three weeks. But most resolutions are forgotten by January 19th and most people can't sustain them. Why can't they sustain those resolutions?

Is their goal vague? Is it abstract? Is it meaningful? Is the reward too far in the future? Did something else better come along the way? Do we even know why we have New Year Resolutions? Supposedly it goes back to ancient Babylonians some 4000 years ago about offering to the gods to pay off debts and have good conduct over the year.

It's important when setting a goal that we are committing to the work put forth in the goal and we acknowledge a change must be made that we want to make. In coaching and as part of my process, we create SMART goals. You may have heard of them as they are used in many experiences. It's an acronym, S M A R T and it stands for

>S=Specific.
>M=Measurable
>A=Achievable
>R=Realistic
>T=Time-Based

Specific means concrete and tangible steps must be taken. *Measurable* reflects how you will know you have completed this goal and you have a tangible result. *Achievable* is being capable of meeting the goal. For example, if your goal is to go ice skating three times a week, you need to be able to skate. *Realistic* must reside in your ability to accomplish the goal with everything else going on in your life. If you work 2 jobs and run around with your kids all weekend, going ice skating 5 days a week is not realistic. Lastly, *Time based* provides the time limit to when you will achieve the goal.

Smart goals allow us to be very clear, very specific in what we want to accomplish.

Here is an example: I want to lose 13 pounds in the next 90 days.

This goal is a smart goal. It's specific and measurable: I want to lose 13 pounds.

It is achievable given that the action steps associated will be exercise and diet. The first five to ten pounds is relatively achievable as well.

In determining if it's realistic, it will need a conversation to determine what else is going on in your life at the time. When I ask the question about it being realistic, that's where we sometimes run into some trouble. So answer this, "Does your situation allow you to do what it's going to take to achieve that goal?" The reality has to be that you have options of going to the gym or that you have equipment at home. You may have a plan to do something that may not require money for the exercise like going for a run.

To break it down a little further with regards to its achievability and being realistic and for you to understand how to approach the creation of your goals, consider that you will need the correct attire; like running shoes, proper exercise attire and etc. If you don't have these items, we may have to create action steps to obtain what you need to achieve the goal.

However, it's important to understand the difference between long term and short-term goals. It is important to set long term goals first, like how it's done in Hollywood where the last scene of a movie is usually filmed first, it's the vision of the accomplished long term goal. We need to shoot your last scene first. Then we put the movie together that ends with that scene. Each scene that leads to the result are the short-term goals.

Goals often require some key action items that will help us achieve that goal. When setting up a smart goal, I like to work with clients and make sure that the longer-term goal, which in this case may be two or three months from now, is that you're going to lose 13 pounds. If you're going to do that, what are the things that need to happen in order for you to do that? What are your action steps?

For example, did you go get running shoes? Did you get exercise attire? Did you get a gym membership? Do you have a gym near you? Answer those questions and then decide in order to lose the 13 pounds these are the key objectives in order to make this happen.

How many times a week are you going to go to the gym? How long are you going to exercise if you choose to go to the gym? Do you go to the gym now, is this something new that you are starting?

Because by creating these smart goals, we will fully understand what we are doing, how to be successful with our main goal and how can we avoid the things that we did in the past that didn't work. So if you have never been to the gym before and you decide you are going to go there three times a week, is that realistic for you?

Because reality might suggest that if you've never been to the gym, you will need to develop a routine before you can do that. What I would encourage a client to do in that situation is say, "Can you go two days before we go three days?" And then we break it down. We look at what are the two days that you can go to the gym? What times can you go? Because for you to succeed in starting that process, you have to have some clear-cut expectations for yourself. Change does not have to be big leaps, but a compilation of small steps.

For example, deciding that you are going to the gym on Saturday and Wednesday at 6:30 am is a good start. It becomes measurable. It becomes an achievable action step. It becomes a realistic goal.

What are the other areas of your life that you want to focus on? Take the issues that we have uncovered/discovered for you and decide the areas that you want to work on. Review the areas that we identified in your exploration as possibilities that you want to explore, create goals to research them.

Is it your relationship? Sometimes it's difficult to put a measurable goal on a relationship. When I work with clients, I try to create an opportunity for them to use a rating scale to give their goal some measurable value. So for example, when I work with people who are struggling in their relationships with their partners and they say they feel that they don't have confidence that they're going to be able to repair their relationship, we use the rating scale. I'll ask them to tell me, "On a scale of one to ten, where would you rate your confidence level in achieving this goal to make your relationship better?" If the number is, say, a 4 on a scale of one to 10, they feel some confidence that they're going to be able to improve their relationship. We set the baseline at four. Then I'll ask, "What do you need for that to move from a four to a six?" We'll talk about some of the action steps that need to happen. Maybe they need to have a regular conversation with their spouse three days a week. Maybe they can do it by sending text messages and work on their communication.

I was meeting with a client and he was struggling to communicate with his wife.

He wants to feel better and more confident about his relationship. I asked, "How do you communicate?" He said, "Well, we just talk." I said, "Well, how do you talk?" And he said, "Well, I tell her what's going on. And then she tells me some stuff that's going on." I then asked if he felt that he was being heard and vice versa. And he said, "No, not really. That's part of what's causing us to drift apart because we don't feel heard." I said to him, "Have you ever heard of active listening?" And he replied, "No." I explained what it was and told him that active listening is basically when someone speaks to you, you repeat in your own words what they just said.

For example, picture a husband and wife having a conversation about how she wants to get a new job. She goes into the whole thing about how she doesn't like her job. She's unhappy where she works. She doesn't like people. She doesn't like the environment that she's in. But she likes some of the work. She likes doing the work. It's important to her. She values that work. The husband's response practicing active listening would say, "I hear you saying that you like what you do but you don't like the environment in which you get to do your job. Do you agree with that statement?"

That is active listening and you can practice it. When he goes to create his goal for them to move the dial from 4 to 6 and to feel confident about his relationship, he will use communication as a way to improve it. His action item is "I want to have three conversations this week with my wife where I use active listening." In addition, he will need to inform his wife of this goal to ensure there is active participation.

That's how we make an ambiguous and relatively vague situation a measurable one, at the same time creating a solid and sophisticated method that is smarter from something that is more subjective.

Now try writing a few goals for yourself. Answer these questions along the way and you will have a SMART Goal.

Write your SMART Goal

1. S: What do you want to change?
2. M: How will you know you accomplished it?
3. A: Are you capable of doing it?
4. R: Does it fit into your everyday life?
5. T: When do you want to accomplish it? What is the date or number of days?

CHAPTER 5

Building the Bridge: Preparing for the Change Work

I have provided insights into making changes and setting goals. One of the things that I find very important is to prepare for change when we are making a choice and the decision to change our lives. It is not easy to prepare for change when it happens for us in a major life transition like losing a job or a loved one. However, it is a matter of perspective in both situations.

Just a quick story about perspective. My daughter Madelyn came home from school one day when she was in Kindergarten and told me that she had several boyfriends. And I turned to her and said, "Do you know what they call a girl with many boyfriends?" and she replied, "Yes, daddy...a GIRLFRIEND!"

Now I share this story because of the difference in our perspectives and when change happens for us or we choose it, there is a need to gain a fresh perspective in our life. We all see change differently and some struggle with it, whereas some move right along with it.

As we begin this chapter, keep the perspective that you are choosing to make a change. I believe that people have to be ready to make a change. As a coach, when I am speaking to a potential client, I am gathering an understanding of the person's motivation to make a change. I'll ask in our Introductory Session, "On a scale of one to ten, how ready are you to make this change in the next 30, 60, 90 days?" People who are motivated will rate it greater than 7. Someone who is a 5 or 6 may not be ready right now, but they may soon. Less than a 5, the person is not ready or in at least my experience, they fail to progress steadily.

We want people who are ready to commit to the process of making change because coaching requires several things. One, it requires work. Two, it requires commitment. Three, it requires an investment of your time and your financial resources.

In this chapter, we are going to explore some of the things that are going to be important in preparing to experience coaching. The point of the preparation is being ready to begin the change process. If you have your mind set to begin this process, it is important to understand what it means to change.

Change is growth. Change is transformation. Change is becoming different.

I created my coaching business and founded it on the concept of the monarch butterfly. The monarch butterfly is such an important symbol of change, transformation, and growth. As you know about metamorphosis, caterpillars enter into a cocoon and after it's gone through growth, pain, discomfort, struggle, whatever it goes through in that cocoon, it comes out as a beautiful butterfly. It expands its wings and is able to soar. That's the change we're speaking about.

The change that we're speaking about, the bridge to change, is overcoming, crossing over, passing through several obstacles along the way to fly out of the cocoon transformed into a bright, elegant, graceful and renewed self, a changed person.

I have a very good friend that commutes to the city. I met him because his son and my son were friends and my wife and his wife became friends. We have a lot of similar interests. We enjoy the same sports and root for the same teams. Our favorite thing to do is recite scenes from the movie, My Cousin Vinny.

These interests have brought us together in friendship. As most friends do, we discuss what's going on in our lives and our work. When he was younger, he worked in a store and learned retail. He eventually became manager. Over his twenty-plus years, he has risen in the organization and works in the corporate office.

There has been a lot of change that has occurred around him. He had several new bosses over the last couple of years due to restructuring. He has been fighting for where he fits and where he belongs. He works long hours and he adapts to the culture. He does everything he can to do the best job possible.

Yet he has been struggling with that role. He has had to set some very clear boundaries. When he commutes on the train in the morning, he would read work emails and start answering them. He would become frustrated. I said to him, "Just stop doing that. Stop looking at your email for work while you're on the train. Create that boundary."

Once 5 o'clock comes, create another boundary. I told him to advise his team not to expect a response from him if they email, to pick up the phone unless it's an emergency and that the best way to reach him in case of an emergency is sending him a text. When we don't set good boundaries, we become discouraged by the things that happen around us. We lose control and become overwhelmed. When we have weak boundaries and we do more than what we need to do and aren't appreciated for it, we become resentful.

I told him, "You have the power to change how you manage your work. Create a boundary. You are at work for 9 hours a day. You need boundaries in order to preserve yourself."

And that's what he did - he stopped looking at his work email on the train, he leaves at 5 pm and he has gotten control back in his life and some more time to spend with his family because of these changes.

You know, a lot of people mock the millennial generation because they have a different work ethic than Gen X'ers and the baby boomers. And yes, it's true, they have a different work ethic, but they are from a different generation. One of the things that I'm always impressed with when I hire a millennial is that they are very good at establishing boundaries.

Who says we have to work more than eight hours at your job? We know the world is changing as companies explore 4-day work weeks. I once had a CEO who used to say to me. "If you get your work done in 30 hours, good for you. If you get it done in 60 hours, that is not good for you. What I am looking for is the impact you make." Decide to create boundaries yet still make an impact. Take this perspective to your work by focusing on making the impact.

When we have weak boundaries, we have weak change or none at all. Boundaries are critical and therefore, they need to be clear in order to make sustainable changes. We must create boundaries in our relationships. I was working with a client recently who's going through a separation. They have two children. The mother of my client is involved in picking up the kids from school. The relationship between my client's wife and his mother is strained at this time. His wife feels that the mother is very involved in their marriage.

I asked him if he considered creating a boundary for his mom. In creating the boundary, we realized that over the course of the week, she only needed to interact with his wife once instead of the 3 times they are now. That boundary will be very important in sustaining the relationship going forward.

Boundaries serve a purpose in creating change. Language is also important.

We have to explore the language we use. It is important to identify the language we use in order to begin change. The use of language is what helps us to live in the positive or the negative. If you are someone who tends to use words like 'can't', 'won't' and 'don't', we have to make some adjustments.

'NOT' is something that should be removed from what we say when we are allowing for life to happen for us. The 'nots' are not part of this conversation. We have to eliminate them.

We must replace them with more positive language. We have to look at what we can do. "What can I do" versus "what I can't do." It is going to take some effort in the beginning, but your awareness of the language you use will change dramatically.

The question must shift to "What can you do? What can you do to move forward? What can you do to take responsibility?" We don't want to use negative language when we are working on changing for the better and creating the positive change, because negative language subconsciously will pull us into a place where we will be held back. It is important to anchor ourselves in a new language. Instead of saying, "I'm not worthy," say, "I am worthy." Or instead of saying, "I'm not deserving" say, "I am deserving."

I am respected. I am good enough. I am changing.

Removing certain language that brings us to a place that doesn't allow us to move forward will result in great success. We have to become cognizant of the things that we're saying on a regular basis. You'll catch yourself now after you've read this. You'll catch yourself saying, "I can't" and you'll change it and say, "I can."

I recently told my staff that I don't make the rules, but I am going to try to live within them. I don't always have the opportunity to choose the work that I will be doing, but I do have the choice on how to complete it. This language changes the perspective on how we will work versus how we won't.

Language is very powerful when people feel that everything happens to them versus for them, because when we come from a place that it's happening to us, everything is, "Why does this happen to me? How come this always happens to me? Why can't I ever get out of this mess?" It's right there in those statements that "I cannot do this". I cannot get out of this mess. But what can you do? All you have to do is take one step forward.

You just have to change one thing. And that's what you can do. You may not be able to resolve everything all at once, but it's what you can do.

My friend also made a choice for a more positive language. He is now posting a positive quote on Instagram every day. When he finds something positive that he relates to, he shares it with me and that encourages us both to move forward. Those are things he is choosing to do. He still has that job. He still goes to work, but he has changed how he looks at it. That's the difference. The shift in his perspective is due to the language that he uses and the boundaries that he set for himself to begin to change.

The next thing you have to be ready for is to answer powerful questions because as a coach it is my role to ask you very powerful ones. You are going to be asked questions that will make you uncomfortable. This is why I often say to people "become comfortable with the uncomfortable" because when we are in a period of change, we are being pushed out of our comfort zone. We are being pushed to question ourselves. We get to question our beliefs, our values, our fears. We question all of those things.

Questions to Consider:

1. What is one boundary you would like to establish?
2. What do you usually say you can't do?
3. How can you change that statement? What can you do?

CHAPTER 6

Different Vehicles that Cross the Bridge: Change as a Spectrum

In business, we often look at a change spectrum when we're going to implement change in an organization. We want to understand how the majority of people will adapt to the implemented changes. There's a curve known as Roger's innovation adoption curve. This model classifies adopters of innovation into various categories. Basically, the categories that people fall into when we approach making change.

Out of 100 people, there will be around 2.5% that usually fall under the category of the innovator. **Innovators** are very brave. They pull the change. They make the change happen. They're very important in communicating things, especially in bringing others along. The next category is the **Early Adopter,** which covers roughly 13.5% of the population. The **Early Adopters** are going to try out the new idea. They're going to go with the flow. They're going to be cautious, but they're going to adopt early. They're going to see the value of the change and say, "Let's try doing it this way."

Then you have the **Early Majority** that makes up about 34 % of the people. They are thoughtful and careful, and they readily accept change more quickly than the average person. Your innovators, early adopters and early majority make up that first 50%. These are the people that are going to help move the change forward.

The other half, the **Late Majority,** are the skeptics. They will use the new idea, but only when the majority is using it. The late majority will wait for the early majority to start doing it, to start working with the change; then they'll do it. The last 16% are considered the **Laggards**. They are traditional people that care for the old ways and are critical towards the new ideas and will only accept it if the new idea has become mainstream or even tradition. The laggard is most resistant to change. You need your innovators and your early majority to pull in the late majority and the late majority to pull in the laggard. It's important to understand where you fall on the spectrum.

This is highly applicable to our coaching relationship. It is part of understanding where you sit on the change spectrum. It is important for you to understand how you make changes in your life. If you're someone who tends to innovate, this is going to be an easier process for you. But if you're someone who waits to see that it works, waits to see that it happens, it's going to be a little bit more difficult for you to get the momentum to start changing.

It's like when a new iPhone comes out. When the new iPhone 11 came out, people were at the door, placing the orders so they would get it as soon as it's available. These are your innovators and your early adopters. Then within a few weeks, everybody in the first half of the spectrum has the new iPhone. This are your early majority. Then there are those people who will wait maybe six months to see if there are kinks that need to be worked out. They don't really want to change their phone yet. That's the late majority.

Then you have the people where the iPhone 11 has been out for two years and they're still on the iPhone 6. These are the laggards. These are the people who are not ready to make that change. Where do you fit on the change spectrum?

I think that it is very important for you to understand and decide where you are. It is going to predict how you adapt to change. It's also going to help me as your coach to understand how I need to work with you in order to pull you along in the change. Will we need to take smaller steps or take leaps and bounds?

Where you sit in regards to this will determine if a goal is achievable and realistic for you. It will be very important for you to understand where you fit on this spectrum.

It is important to note that this may be situationally dependent for you. For example, if your goal is to begin exercising again after a 3-month hiatus, you will probably jump back into it faster than someone who has never exercised before. Previous experience may allow you to be an Early Adopter whereas no experience may make you more cautious and therefore may classify you as either early or late majority. There are some areas of your life where you will be more willing to join the early majority and others where you may be lagging behind.

Questions to Consider:

1. Which group do you feel you belong on the spectrum of change?
2. Do you live in that group most of the time or some of the time?
3. Think of different areas of your life. Which areas do you live in the innovator, early adopter or early majority? Which areas do live in the late majority or laggards?

CHAPTER 7

There's Roadwork on the Bridge: Blocks and Obstacles

As we move forward in coaching, there is going to be a lot of conversation about running into blocks and obstacles and of course your fears will pop up and get in the way of you moving forward. Values and beliefs will surface and cause some of these blocks as well. Therefore, I devoted chapter 3 to identifying your core values and beliefs. In order to move forward, you need to know what they are and when they will rear their potentially ugly head in your movement forward. They may be the cause for you to stop moving. One of the things that we're going to need to do is determine how to work on those blocks and obstacles.

Some blocks are easier to work on than others. We can resolve some blocks by taking action. We can put a plan in place on what we are going to do to get you moving forward. However, not all blocks can be solved by action. Some require an internal approach. Many of our fears are inner blocks. However not all inner blocks are fears. Some examples of the inner blocks are beliefs and assumptions that we have of ourselves, like self-worth, self-respect and the feeling of not being good enough.

Sometimes they are subconscious blocks that we don't realize that we're putting out there. It may be related to prior experiences. It may be something that we're feeling like judgment. It could be the inability to forgive ourselves. It's living with regret. It's having an approach that is not in line with the positive perspective that we're trying to attain.

Maybe it's related to a negative experience. In preparing for change, we have to understand that we're going to encounter these issues or feelings.

When my clients want to move forward toward a goal and another part of them wants to stay back, we do a technique by Dr. Hal and Sidra Stone called Voice Dialogue. Voice dialogue helps us as coaches to move someone forward when they're truly stuck. There is a battle between the two parts of the client that results in inertia. Until we try to integrate the two aspects, whether it's we want to move forward versus we don't want to move forward, we can't move forward.

For example, let's say you have a career mom that wants to move forward in her career but being a mom is holding her back. She wants to be that perfect career mom. And so instead of figuring out what those things are that she needs to move forward, she's getting stuck in her own way because she cannot differentiate how to step forward to be both mom and career woman.

We start by labeling these two parts. Then we ask a series of questions revolving around what the two parts need from each other and want to give to each other. In this case the career woman and the mom would each be part. And in this activity, we break down some of the barriers.

Then the client picks an inanimate object that represents each part, the career and being a mom. The client then visualizes those two inanimate objects working together. At the end, if it's done effectively, it helps us to gain understanding of how to integrate the two parts together. If we're able to integrate those two parts together in a more powerful way, in a way that's more concrete and clearer, it helps the client to move forward. But in that process of talking about being a career woman versus being a mom, we're breaking down what those blocks are. When everything is broken down, she can recognize that she is the same person and those parts can integrate and work together to find the fulfillment she is looking for.

Another block that many of my clients experience is judgment. Every time I sit down with someone for the first time, I usually tell them that this is a place where judgment does not exist. I do not want judgment to block me from helping someone to move forward. My clients all know that when they come into my office or speak to me over a video session, there is no judgment from me. I am not here to judge. I am here to be a cheerleader, to support you through your changes, to support you in moving forward and not be focused on the judgment that people have put on you that have gotten you to this point.

Judgment is a powerful block. It's something that we face often because we are judged constantly. We are judged all the time – by our employers, our friends, our family. It is very important in the coaching process to remove that judgment because by doing so, it allows us to really be truthful about who we are. If you are too hard on yourself, you are your own worst judge.

Understanding the role that judgment plays in your life is going to be critical in taking the steps forward that you need to take. Imagine if the world was not a judgmental place. Imagine if we gave up whether or not there is right or wrong and there's just ways that people choose. Imagine if we eliminated that judgment.

People would live more freely. People would have less strain in their lives. Judgment also becomes a blind spot. It commits us to a decision; it blocks us sometimes in our ability to see the truth. It can be disruptive. It can make us contribute to a non-truth, so when we talked about beliefs earlier, we talked about the importance of validating them. Beliefs and assumptions formed in judgment are blocks too.

I have a client that is in her 20's. She is miserable in her job. She is making a salary that is very good for her experience. However, she wants to change career paths and thus she wants to quit. She lives at home with her parents and has few bills and responsibilities. However, her parents are very vocal about her life, imposing their beliefs and inserting their fears in her life. This is blocking her from moving forward. But the key block is how she feels judged by her father. His judgment is shaking her foundation. It is stopping her from moving forward. His judgment is blinding him to help her explore the other opportunities that she can choose.

Judgment is important to understand as a block. If you have the ability to take a step back and remove judgment, especially judgment of yourself, you will be more successful. When we stop judging others, we become less judgmental of ourselves because we stop comparing ourselves to others.

When we compare ourselves to others, we are judging ourselves against a false standard. I have a client in his late 20's and he's feeling unsuccessful because he doesn't have a girlfriend right now. He lives at home with his parents, but his friends all have girlfriends and they're getting married and they have their own places to live. He's taking that situation and comparing himself to them. He's judging himself and creating false standards based on other people. He is so wrapped up in seeing what he doesn't have, that he can't see what he does have. He is not able to see the truth about himself and that this is his journey. He does not accept that he is right where he needs to be right now. Until he removes that judgment, his blind spots will continue to be present.

When we gossip, we judge. Gossip is as contagious as the flu; it spreads quickly and hurts our immune system and hurts our emotional well-being. It hurts who we are.

It brings negative energy out. If we gossip, we're passing judgment. If we gossip, it's because we're not looking at our own issues that need work. We're blinding ourselves to our own truths when we gossip. It creates more judgment. We're passing more judgment, and if we don't want to be judged, we have to stop passing judgment on others.

As Joel Osteen often says, "The only person that you have to compare yourself to is the person you were yesterday." Am I better than I was yesterday? And if I'm not, what do I need to do to move myself forward? What do I need to do differently in order to be better than I was yesterday? Only focus on comparing yourself to yourself from one day to the other.

Don't compare yourself to other people. Don't go on social media and think you're going to get in touch with your own truth by seeing what everybody else is doing. Visit your mirror, look yourself in the eyes and scroll through you. Taking inventory of how you are, what beliefs you have, what affirmations you recite and compare yourself to yourself from yesterday. That's going to be your new comparison.

You have to recognize, too, that it's OK to take care of you. It's OK to be selfish in a loving way, a self-loving way. Take care of oneself, be true to who you are. It's OK to put yourself first. When you go through this process of rediscovering who you are and changing who you are because you have a desire to do things differently, it's okay to be focused just on you. Don't miss out on you. Don't be 10 years down the road and say, "I wish I had spent the time to change". Don't miss out on you while you're comparing yourself to someone else on social media. Focus on you. Focus on what you're doing right here and right now. Again, be present right now. That's what it takes to move forward.

Remove the judgment. Remove the gossip. Remove the blocks and obstacles. Patch up the potholes. You have finished the roadwork, move forward focusing on the question, "Are you better today than you were yesterday?"

Questions to Consider:

1. What judgments impact me the most?
2. Do I make many judgments about others?
3. What blocks or obstacles am I aware of?
4. Who do I compare myself to and why?
5. What part of me wants to move forward, and what part is holding me back?
6. Am I better today than I was yesterday?

CHAPTER 8

Crossing the Bridge: Incremental Action Steps

We all develop incrementally just as we witness in the development of a child. We have developmental milestones that we measure in the first years of our lives to make sure that we are progressing and growing to reach our full potential. That's how we're built. We're built to do things incrementally. It is the same with change.

Change doesn't happen overnight. It is a process, a journey that requires time. Creating sustainable change requires time.

A coaching session is how we begin crossing the bridge. It's in the sessions that we do the work and prepare action steps to keep you moving forward. In every session, I will ask you, "What do you want to work on today?" The second question is,

"What would you like to accomplish by the end of our session?" It is in these 2 questions that we work on the goals, review the accomplishments, identify the blocks and obstacles and create a plan to integrate or remove them so that you keep moving forward.

People are overwhelmed often by the number of things that they have to accomplish. They perceive having too much to do and when they feel this, they avoid doing them, procrastinating. In order to improve on this, we need to break the work down into bite-size pieces instead of mouthfuls. In breaking down what needs to be done, we make it more tangible and easier to accomplish. When we take a small thing and we add it to our routine, it becomes more sustainable.

In an earlier chapter, I spoke about a husband and wife who are struggling with their communication. We created a small change to utilize the skills of active listening, a skill that takes practice. However, in order to make that sustainable we have to incrementally introduce it into each conversation. So let us start small. Utilizing three out of 10 conversations over the course of the week is an incremental change. Once that goal has been achieved, we can increase it to 4 or 5 then 6, 8, all the time. Eventually the communication should be so sound that they'll be doing active listening without even realizing that they're doing it.

When you choose to do something new and it becomes part of what you do, you never know how you did it in the past. Correct? People say that all the time when they have children. I don't know how we did that before we had children because children will force you to change. When you have children, you have to follow a process to get your kids out of the house. You have to follow a process to go somewhere. You first learn with baby number one that you have to pack up the baby bag, the pack and play, the food bag, etc. You learn some things the hard way, but then you find your groove. As the baby grows, you start reducing what you bring with you when you have to go somewhere. You make adjustments at each step of the way.

Some of them are bigger than others, but you made incremental changes as the child developed. That's how you have to look at this approach. This approach and these action steps are synonymous with the development of a child. When pushing toward each milestone, there are challenges to overcome. As they change step by step, you must acknowledge, too, that you can only change so much so fast. If you are not capable, if you don't have the muscle strength to stand up, you're going to have to crawl for a little while. And that's what we focus on in creating these action plans.

I had a client come to me and say that one of his goals was to go to the gym 5 days a week. Although an ambitious goal, is it sustainable? So I asked him, "How many days do you currently visit the gym every week?" He replied, "None." He was running before he even crawled. So how do we create sustainable change here? In addition to setting the SMART goal, which he changed to a long-term goal of 4 days a week based on his lifestyle, we must create the action steps for incremental change, thus creating sustainability.

In our session, we worked on getting him to go 2 days a week to start and the goal would be that this would be accomplished over the course of 4 weeks before increasing it to 3 times a week. He accomplished his goals. He got to 4 days a week and has sustained that for several months now. But it's in the success of each milestone, the realistic approach, the incremental steps that make it sustainable.

It is going to be very successful when you've done it incrementally. Sometimes we're going to have to change that up. It's OK to have some setbacks. It's OK to take a step back, but that's where the accountability piece is going to come in as an important factor in the change process.

Are you doing the work to make the change? You tried something and it didn't work. How are you responding to that? However, if you didn't make the attempts, that is a different conversation.

When you want to change and you don't do the work to change, a coach will hold you accountable. I'm going to ask you, "What is getting in your way? What are the distractions happening around you that are not allowing you to take the steps?" That's the approach that we're going to take as you create action steps. Take one step at a time, be present in the moment, it's small steps at a time you can accomplish.

Athletes that run a marathon don't go out and run the 26.2 miles in the first run. They start with a few miles and each week increase how many miles they run a day. They develop the muscle, lung and physical capacity to do it. If they don't start out running a few miles and increase over time, they won't accomplish their goal. See each block or obstacle as the muscle soreness, a temporary phase, in developing the muscle to where it needs to be. Be patient and wait until you develop a little bit more and then continue forward. It is meant to be uncomfortable moving out of your comfort zone.

This is a process of continuous improvement. It's making small changes and making sure they stick. And as it becomes more routine, we create more sustainable change.

You don't have to make dramatic leaps and bounds to start your progress forward. That's why coaching is recommended to be a yearlong process because sustainable changes take time. We have to work towards something and we have to do it in small steps. That's why we also create long term goals and then we use short term goals to accomplish them.

Remember, you have to crawl before you can walk and you have to walk before you can run.

Questions to Consider:

1. What is a small change that you can make?
2. What will be the next change to add once you have made a small change?
3. Is there a third small change in your process that needs to be added? What is it?
4. What adjustments do you need to make after each step to achieve your goal?

CHAPTER 9

Paying the toll: The Value of Your Work

Now that we are getting into the routine of your coaching, we need to check the value of your work. The more you put in, the more you get out of it. If you are not putting in any effort, then this process will not work for you and change will not occur.

Having perseverance is critical to this process. As things come up, whether block, obstacle, fear, set-back, etc., you must persevere in the task. It is part of making the commitment to the process. It is the old adage of "when the going gets tough, the tough gets going."

Our main goal is to add value to your life. Therefore, it is important that we spend time on what you desire to see change. This is an important commitment and you must see value in what we are trying to accomplish because coaching should be a valuable life-changing experience.

For example, a few months ago, I was working with a client who was not willing to put the work in to make the changes that she desired to make. We will call her Rose. Rose is in her sixties; she has 2 sons and their relationship has a strong emphasis on the financial dependence of her children. They are in their thirties and she still provides a lot of financial support. She doesn't have the best of relationships with one of her sons because she is highly skeptical about his wife.

She doesn't like this woman who seems to take advantage of her son and the support that Rose provides to them. In one of our sessions, she wanted to work on "her diet when she goes to visit her son". More specifically, she did not like that every time she visits, they only go to eat fast food. In this case, she spoke about ordering a hamburger at McDonald's, something she prefers not to eat.

While working with her during that session, every question I asked about options she could choose as an alternative to the hamburger was "No, I don't think I can do that. " She had an excuse for everything. She was skirting the real issue.

What she was really doing was demonstrating how uncomfortable she is when she visits her son. She was making the session about not eating a hamburger because she was avoiding the issue for what she needed to work on. But she demonstrated how she had a loss of control over the situation. She was not choosing an alternative because she was stuck. The time we spent on the hamburger, we could have been discussing the real issues.... the ones that will add true value to her relationships and change her life.

People will substitute things so that they don't have to deal with the issues that they really need to deal with. The only person who limits us on moving forward is ourselves. My client was limiting herself and avoiding work. She was fearful of what the work meant for her. When I asked her if she really wanted to change the relationship, she decided to end the coaching relationship. Her motivation was not there, and she was not ready to change.

When someone is motivated and perseveres through the process, incredible things happen that provide great value to your life. Take the following story about a client of mine who is going through a separation from his wife.

My client reached out to me when he learned of his wife's infidelity. At first, he was willing to stay in the marriage and do whatever it takes to fix it. However, his motivator for doing this is because of his fear of being alone. He was willing to stay in a relationship where he had lost trust, honesty, and love because of fear.

During our sessions, he would come with changes he wanted to make, but the fear was not being integrated. The fear moved from being alone to losing everything he had financially. He came to one session and said how the fear was getting worse. He was very afraid of being alone. I said, "What do you need at the end of this session in order for us to move you forward?" He replied, "I need some way to meet new people." Then we worked on what it was that he could do.

He didn't know exactly what he wanted to do at first. I asked what would hold him back from just going out and having conversations with people, anyone who he met. He could have passed on that question and done nothing with it, but he decided to create a goal to have conversations with random people and taking a chance on different apps, which led to having coffee with someone he met, and now it became a friendship he didn't have before. That's what happens when you take a step and do the work. He made the effort, the fear is there, but not as prominent as it was before because he has overcome the first step to integrating the fear into his life. He acted.

He also realized how easy it was for him to meet new people which also made the fear dissipate. What was the work he did to add value to his life? One, he was embracing that he needed to make a change in order to integrate his fear. Two, it was acknowledging that his fear existed and he was willing to work on it. Three, he was willing to take the step forward and he was willing to make a change. He was willing to put himself out there. He realized when he took the steps forward; it was beneficial. It showed him that it was not as difficult as he was making it out to be. He was crossing the bridge to change. Four, he allowed himself to be free and not worry about being judged and not judging himself.

This is a lot of the same work that many of my clients do. We explore where things are getting in the way and we don't say to get rid of them. We work on integrating them. We work on making them part of what we're going to carry along the way. Whether it's a fear or a block, or obstacle, we make them part of what informs us.

If you are willing to make those changes and talk about those things, you will have a successful coaching experience.

As you put in the work, I want you to be aware of the things that come up for you in doing that, because identifying what comes up for you when you're working on a goal is where your self-awareness develops even further. Your self-awareness comes to the forefront because you start to realize why you may be avoiding something or not dealing with it. As you do the work and improve your self-awareness, you start to recognize that crutch or that fear or what has stopped you from moving forward in the past. The important thing to remember is when issues come up for you, you refrain from judging yourself.

It is important to be kind to yourself during this process. Are you allowing yourself to be forgiven? Forgiveness is a very important part of being able to move forward. A lot of times when we are struggling to move forward on something it's because we haven't forgiven ourselves. If I can forgive myself, I have removed the judgment of myself. I'm allowing myself to move forward in a forgiven state.

Another important roadblock that comes up in this process is the matter of trusting in the process. Many of my clients that have been successful in implementing changes in their life will tell you to trust in the process. Allow for the things that are going to happen for you to happen.

People tend to be unsuccessful in achieving their goals when they don't trust in the process. You have to trust, not just the process, but that you can make the changes. When you start to trust that this is happening for you, that it's happening for your growth, development, and metamorphosis, you transform. You become that beautiful butterfly.

Consider what we do when we experience an illness. We have to put our trust in the provider that's taking care of us to help cure the sickness. This past year, I had surgery. My illness was holding me back in doing the things that I needed to do in my life. I had gone back and forth out of fear whether I would have the surgery, however, I had to embrace that this too was happening for me.

I put trust out there that the surgeon was going to take the best care of me. When I put my trust, not just in the surgeon, but in the fact that I had to go through a healing process, it was the thing that allowed me to move forward and to be able to be here right now writing this book. It was the thing that has taken me in the first two months of a new year to new heights with the clients that I work with because I put trust, I put trust that this had to happen for me. And when I trusted, I was rewarded.

I love the word 'disease'. People have disease. Disease is what holds them back from living healthy and productive lives. But what I love about this word is the meaning behind what it is. It is a dis-ease.

When we have dis-ease, we are not comfortable, we are uneasy. It is a time that pain and suffering may occur but we are probably learning to grow. In the dis-ease process, healing takes place.

The coaching journey, your bridge to change, is about healing. When we want to change something, we often have to get rid of what is diseased. Like my client Rose, she has to experience dis-ease if she is going to improve her relationship with her son. We have to trust that it's happening for us and we have to face that we may experience some dis-ease.

You will grow, you will transform and you will fly like that butterfly.

As we work at this process you let go of the things that don't serve you. This allows you to change. Whatever doesn't serve you, whether it be people, a job, a spouse, a friendship - these are the things that may cause you dis-ease. If you put in the work and remove these diseased pieces, you add value to the work and the changes you are making.

People need to feel that they have been embraced so that they have some comfort going through the uncomfortable. That's my role as a coach. My role is to help you through the dis-ease, to support you.

It's your process, not mine, but it is a process where I can join you. I can meet you in what you're doing and where you are in that stage of life. We work to achieve your goals. When we do the work, trust the process, that's when we move forward and improve our self-awareness.

Questions to Consider:

1. Are you doing the work to make the changes you truly seek to make?
2. Do you need someone to hold you accountable because you are not accomplishing your goals?
3. Do you trust in the process?
4. Do you see your self-awareness changing?
5. What is the dis-ease you are affected by?

CHAPTER 10

Continuing the Journey: Sustaining the Change

~~~

As we discussed throughout the course of this book, the goal here is to create sustainable change for life fulfillment. We talked about it being incremental. We talked about making it part of your regular routine. We've talked about all the different aspects of what goes into change and being able to make a change.

Now we come to the point where we must evaluate and ask, Have the changes been made? Have they been made successfully? Are they sustainable? Have you integrated your fears? Are your beliefs consistent with your values? You will need to re-evaluate this every now and again.

Making incremental change really allows us to move towards a more sustainable change. Change, in the beginning, tends to be more dramatic than at other points. Sometimes we will hit a plateau on that bridge to change as we cross over it. We may come to a flat road once we've reached the changes that we're happy with. When you are evaluating where you are, ask these questions: Am I in a good place? Have the decisions that you made resulted in the changes you wanted? Are you better today than you were yesterday because you made these changes?

Accepting the plateau is up to you.

Keep a fresh perspective on change. You've become much more self-aware. You probably have become a little bit more self-aware just by reading this book. But being self-aware and keeping a fresh perspective and how you view change is going to be important in your ability to change in the future.

You may have setbacks along the way but it is imperative to persevere, which will allow you to sustain your changes. When you struggle, come back to this book, read it again to be reminded of what to do when you lose focus, get lost, or struggle to make a change.

My job is not to make myself a crutch for you to lean on as a coach and no coach is going to ever want to be a crutch for you to lean on. We are here to help you go through a process so that when other things happen for you in your life and when change happens for you, you have been equipped with the tools that you need to embrace that change.

I've been told in the past, "You know, you've changed. You're different." The tone used is negative. I often look at the people that say that to me and realize that they are afraid to make the changes in their life. They are not any different than they were the last time we saw each other. No different than they were five years ago. We have to remember that change is a part of life. It is something that is going to happen. We can't always control that. And why not change?

Remember that when you change, you are changing to evolve, to grow, to transform and to be a better version of you. We strive to be better today than we were yesterday. That is the change you are trying to achieve.

At this point, you have either shifted levels of consciousness from Level 1 to Level 2 or more convinced that you live in Level 2. You embrace that change happens for you. Now the goal is to make it happen through you, to move back and forth between Level 2 and Level 3.

You can take this experience and what you've read in this book to help someone else make changes as well. Be that person who can say to someone you know, "I made some changes in my life and I feel better because of it." It is a process that requires a lot of work and commitment but the bridge to self-awareness is worth it. Be there for someone else and cheer them on through their changes to be a better version of themselves. Take that opportunity to have change happen through you because it is through you that you also reaffirm your own changes.

Coaching is not a one-method approach that works for everyone. Coaching must be adjusted depending on the person. I learned with my experiences that I couldn't approach every client the same way. There are many ways to bring someone across the bridge to change. It is not one standard route. There is no right or wrong as long as you get to the other side of the bridge.

Take the things that you have learned from here to move forward towards becoming your more authentic self. Live your truth. Be who you are as a person. Live free of judgment.

Hold yourself accountable for your long-term successes and your happiness.

You will find fulfillment when you approach change in a positive way. You will find fulfillment when you remove judgment of yourself. You can hold yourself accountable without judging. Always be open to recognizing your truth and maintaining your truth. It's in knowing yourself well enough, that you will recognize when change is necessary.

The experiences you have on your journey are going to inform you, raise your self-awareness, and give you new perspectives. You will be pushed outside of your comfort zone and will be forced to create new boundaries. Use the discomfort and your willingness to make the change as your motivator.

If you do those things, you will live truthfully. You will live free.

Honor your values and make sure that they are in everything that you do. Whether you enter a relationship, new job, change a career, meet people, experience a loss, experience a major life transition; be sure that you accept that it's happening for you. Remember to re-evaluate your values. Be honest with your belief systems and understand that your beliefs and values are going to change. They have to change in order for us to evolve.

Keep going no matter what. Keep moving forward. Yes, there's going to be some blips along the road across the bridge.

There's going to be a couple of potholes from those bad storms you may weather. But you're going to pass through those, you're going to pass over those. It's going to happen, but it's in how you respond that matters. It's your reaction when you swerve to avoid that pothole. That is going to make all the difference.

Lastly, don't let fear hold you back. Let fear be what it is - a protector, a guide, an informer. You don't have to let go of the fear, honor and integrate it in your steps forward. Let it be the bumps in the road next to the guiding yellow line that stops you from going off the bridge.

You have crossed the bridge to change, keep moving forward to a life of fulfillment!

BONUS CHAPTER

The SMARTER Method for Setting Priorities and Resolving Issues

Many people struggle with organizing their lives, prioritizing the things that are most important and accomplishing the things they want to achieve. There are various strategies that focus on time management, one of these is making a checklist to provide order in your life. In her book, Attention Management, Maura Thomas discusses that if we control our attention and give the right amount of attention to a project or our priorities, we can accomplish goals and lead more productive lives.

We also know that when attempting to accomplish something, we must avoid procrastinating on the things that are important. One of the key elements to reducing our procrastination is making sure our goals are specific as opposed to vague.

When I work with clients on their time management, attention management and organizing their issues, we set SMART goals that become the foundation of our work together. We discussed these in Chapter 4, however here is a refresher. SMART goals refer to goals that are specific, measurable, achievable, realistic and time-based. In coaching, I walk you through how to formulate SMART goals to help you organize and prioritize what it is that you want to achieve.

However, in the context of organizing your life, improving your time and attention management, and achieving your goals, I would like to offer you the SMARTER method to prioritize tasks or resolve issues. With the SMARTER method, you will be able to differentiate between what is important, what attention and resources will be needed, how much of your energy will be demanded and ensure you are focused on the reward for your efforts.

When approaching your list of issues or tasks that you need to prioritize be sure to ask yourself the questions associated with each letter:

S = Is this something that I Should Do? Is the task at hand something that I should do? What happens if I don't complete the task or resolve the issue? Is there a major consequence or a minor one? If it is major, it shifts to the next letter, M. If it has a minor consequence, then it is something that I should do. For example, finishing the laundry today, when you have enough clothes for tomorrow, would result in a minor consequence or none at all if you put it off until the next day.

M = Is this something that I MUST do? This is something that has a MAJOR consequence if you don't complete it. For example, if you don't file your taxes you may be fined by the IRS or face other severe consequences. Or if you don't pay your mortgage, you will find yourself in foreclosure at some point. These are major consequences.

A = Your level of Attention that is required. The more important the task, the more important it is to understand the level of attention that will be needed to accomplish it. Attention required will vary and may not be predictive of the significance of the task or issue, however, it will help you to prioritize what you will be able to do that day or moment based on your level of attention. If something requires your attention and you need to be focused, but you are distracted, you may need to re-prioritize the task or issue. You may defer to the one that requires less attention. If this means the MUST do task will not be accomplished because it requires a high level of attention, then ask for assistance or take a minute to clear your mind and refocus your attention.

R = Resources needed to accomplish the task or issue. When prioritizing tasks or issues, you will need to account for the resources that it requires. Does it require money, other people, things that you have, etc.? Basically, do you have what you need? Having the right resources will determine how achievable it will be for you to accomplish the task or resolve the issue.

T = Give yourself enough Time. As with SMART Goals, there is a reference to time, however, the difference here is how much time will it take you to accomplish the task or to resolve the issue. If you are struggling to prioritize two issues that are MUST do situations, then the amount of time one may take will help you decide which to do first.

E = Your Energy to complete the task or resolve your issues. Are you physically and mentally energetic? Is this something that requires physical energy or mental energy? Are you exhausted either physically or mentally? Your level of energy will be important to accomplishing your task. Again, use this to guide how you reprioritize the MUST do issue and make sure you have the energy it takes.

R = Instant or Delayed Reward? What is the benefit of completing the task or resolving the issue? Will the reward be immediate, or will it be further in the future? Understanding when you will reap the benefits of your work will help you in persevering towards accomplishing the task or resolving the issue. If you don't consider this, you may be more inclined to procrastinate on the matter.

In summary, when you attempt to organize your life, improve prioritizing tasks and issues to resolve, and improve your time and attention management, follow the SMARTER method:

S	M	A	R	T	E	R
Should Do	Must Do	Attention	Resources	Time	Energy	Reward

THANK YOU FOR READING MY BOOK!

FREE BONUS GIFT

Just to say thanks for buying and reading my book, I would like to give you a free bonus gift that will add value and that you will appreciate, 100% FREE, no strings attached!

To Download Now, Visit:

http://www.bridgetochangebook.com/TM/freegift

I appreciate your interest in my book and I value your feedback as it helps me improve future versions of this book. I would appreciate it if you could leave your invaluable review on Amazon.com with your feedback. Thank you!

NORTH MERRICK PUBLIC LIBRARY
1691 MEADOWBROOK ROAD
NORTH MERRICK, NY 11566

JAN 07 2021

Made in the USA
Columbia, SC
03 June 2020

Donation 1/7/21

98156478R00078